Noah and the Giant

Dan and Marie Nolting

WestBow Press books may be ordered through booksellers or by contacting:

WestBow Press
A Division of Thomas Nelson & Zondervan
1663 Liberty Drive
Bloomington, IN 47403
www.westbowpress.com
844-714-3454

Because of the dynamic nature of the Internet, any web addresses or links contained in this book may have changed since publication and may no longer be valid. The views expressed in this work are solely those of the author and do not necessarily reflect the views of the publisher, and the publisher hereby disclaims any responsibility for them.

Any people depicted in stock imagery provided by Getty Images are models, and such images are being used for illustrative purposes only. Certain stock imagery © Getty Images.

Interior Image Credit: Ellen Thomas

ISBN: 979-8-3850-4254-8 (sc)
ISBN: 979-8-3850-4255-5 (hc)
ISBN: 979-8-3850-4253-1 (e)

Library of Congress Control Number: 2025901116

Print information available on the last page.

WestBow Press rev. date: 02/12/2025

WestBow
PRESS®
A DIVISION OF THOMAS NELSON
& ZONDERVAN

Noah and the Giant

Dedication

This book is dedicated to all of the Grandchildren and Grandparents looking to connect in a fun and creative way! While playing with my own grandson Noah, I found that one of the most important roles a Grandparent can play in the development of a child's life is to show them that their imagination can span generations and that we can all connect with someone on some level. My Grandson and I had a typical relationship... mind your parents, play catch, pick up your toys etc.. until one day at the lake with just the two of us. We were taking a swim together and just like the start of the book I emerged from the water pretending to be a Giant who was going to toss him in the lake. Noah's eyes lit up and he immediately connected on a different level with an excited focus! We played, laughed and connected in a way we had not yet to date. To this day (many years later), my Grandkids continue to ask for "the Giant".. can you go get the Giant Bop? I have to leave the room, take off my glasses, change something and emerge with a deep voice like a giant from another land! Our time with them is short... be a little bit parent, a little bit teacher and a little bit Giant!

The Giant (aka Bop and Mrs Giant, aka Rie Rie)...

Noah was playing down by the water one day (being careful and wearing his swim vest of course), when he heard rustling along the shoreline nearby....

"*Hello*".. Noah hesitantly whispered....

"*Grumph*"... he heard in reply..

Noah, being a confident and brave little boy again proclaimed "*Hello? Do you need help in there?*"..

With that, a real life Giant stepped out from behind the trees and bushes and bellowed "*I'm a Giant... how could a little thing like you help me?!?*"

"*Well*".... Said Noah, "*I'm a pretty good swimmer, I know how to catch fish and I know a lot about animals?*"

The Giant said, "*I know all those things.. now unless you can give me something, go away or ill toss you into the lake!*"

Noah thought quickly and said, "*well Giant.. maybe I can't give you any of those things, but I can be your friend??*"

1

The Giant sat for a minute musing at the tiny boy.. "and what exactly is a friend?"

Noah answered.. "Well, we do fun things together... we look out for each other.. we share our things like toys and snacks.. we play and run and jump and swim and just have fun!...".

"Hrumph" the Giant said.. "I've never had one of those before.... I like you little critter!"

Noah laughed "I'm not a critter, I'm a little boy.. and your best friend Giant!"

The Giant felt something in his heart he had never felt before... he liked being with this little boy and decided he would learn about what it was like to be a little boy, as well as teach Noah all about Giant things! They high fived and made it official!

When Noah went home that night, he told his Mommy and Daddy all about the nice Giant he had met..

"That's very nice Noah, we're glad you made another friend" now we need you to finish your dinner so that you can get ready for bed."

After Dinner, Noah asked his Daddy if he could read him a bedtime story about a Giant.. his Daddy said "unfortunately we don't have any books about Giants, but we'll certainly look for one for another day"..

The next morning, Noah heard a familiar "Rumph" as he was slowly waking from a good night sleep.. he looked over and saw the face of the Giant fogging up his second story window!

"Hello little friend" the Giant said.. *"can you come out and go exploring?"*

Noah jumped out of bed, got dressed, brushed his teeth, ate his breakfast and sped to the back yard where the Giant was patiently waiting..

The Giant scooped up his little friend, tossed him on his shoulder and off they went, covering ground faster than Noah could believe. Noah was sitting up so high he could see everything!

The Giant asked *"What is that over there?"* pointing to his school.

"That's my School" said Noah..

"What is a School? Can I eat it?" quipped the Giant..

"Nooo", laughed Noah, *"that's where we go to learn about the world and each other".*

"Oh" said Giant.. *"What about that over there asked Giant... Can I eat those?"* pointing to the cars on the local car lot.

"Noooo", said Noah, *"those are cars that we use to get around in"..*

"Hrumph" said the Giant...

Noah, realizing the Giant was VERY hungry told the Giant to head down a country road. Making quick time of the journey, they ended up at Molinari Farm, where Noah and his family went to get fresh vegetables. Noah explained to the Giant, *"This is s farm, where our food comes from"*..

The Giant, giddy with excitement said *"what can we eat?.. How about that critter?"* pointing to a tractor.

"Haha, no Giant! That is a tractor used for plowing the fields"..

"Hrumph" said the Giant.... *"How about those things over there?"* pointing to a wheel barrow and some tools..

"Nope" said Noah... *"but I will show you some things that we can eat Giant"*

They walked out along the edge of the fence where there was a large field of silver queen corn growing. *"Try a few of these Giant"* Noah said.. *"These are called silver queen corn and are delicious"..*

The Giant grabbed a few stalks and started plucking off the ears eating them whole. *"Giant likes this! We have something similar in Giantland called Glorg"* *"MMMMMM"...*

Silver Queen Corn

11

"*Not too many Giant.. now come over here*" said Noah leading the Giant to a patch of pumpkins.. "*We make Pie and bread and delicious muffins out of these and they are called pumpkins*"..

Giant grabbed a few and chomped on them like they were apples.... "*Hahaha*" Noah laughed, "*You sure like to eat Giant!*"

Next Noah took the Giant to a field where there were apple trees as far as the eye could see. *"these are more delicious superfood called apples"….*

The Giant shook the tree with one hand and held out his other hand and filled it full of apples falling off the tree. He threw a handful into his mouth like grapes and chomped away. *"These are very good proclaimed the Giant".*.

"Do you have anything like this in Giantland" asked Noah….

"Why yes we do… they are called Lorbles and are much larger and purple in color". Said the Giant.

Well Giant, I better get back to my house because my mommy will be making my lunch soon.. The two sped back across the country side, into town and over the fence into Noah's back yard in no time.

"Thank you friend for teaching Giant about so many things today" said the Giant....

"Your Welcome Giant.. maybe you can come back tomorrow and we can play some more?" "Tomorrow Giant want to take friend Noah to Giant Land and teach him about Glorg, and Porples and Luttles...". Said the Giant.

The Giant sure liked having a friend in Noah, and Noah sure liked the Giant and teaching him about his world.

"OK, Giant.. tomorrow we go to Giantland! I'll see you at my window when I wake up!"

"OK, little buddy, Giant will be here and will make sure my little friend Noah is safe and sound.."

With that, The Giant stepped over the fence and walked off waving to his best friend with a warm heart and excitement for the next day's adventure!

Printed in the United States
by Baker & Taylor Publisher Services